EXPRESS YOURSELF!

written by Linda Lee Maifair
illustrated by Priscilla Burris

LINDA LEE MAIFAIR received a Bachelor of Science degree and two Master of Education degrees in reading and English from Indiana University of Pennsylvania. As a certified reading specialist, her background includes creative writing for young children and teens in children's magazines and writing for other educational publishers. As a freelance writer and consultant, she teaches creative writing classes at Wilson College in Chambersburg, Pennsylvania.

PRISCILLA BURRIS received an Associate of Arts degree in Creative Design from the Fashion Institute of Design and Merchandising in Los Angeles. As a freelance artist of child-related artwork, she has been drawing since she was one year old. Priscilla lives in southern California.

Copyright 1988 by **THE MONKEY SISTERS, INC.**
22971 Via Cruz
Laguna Niguel, CA 92677

ISBN 0-933606-57-5

TO THE TEACHER

The language arts lessons in EXPRESS YOURSELF! give students the opportunity to express themselves in written, oral and artistic ways.

The five questions in each **THINK ABOUT/TALK ABOUT** section may be part of a class discussion or may be used as a written assignment to give students practice in writing complete sentences.

The **WRITE ABOUT** section is designed to foster paragraph writing and creative writing. A series of questions are presented, and students may answer these in sequence to develop their paragraph/s or may take a more creative approach and incorporate the answers in their own way. For students who have difficulty writing paragraphs, the method of answering the questions sequentially, in sentences, will give them success in developing complete paragraphs.

PICTURE THIS is designed to provide a fun and artistic way to complete the language arts lessons.

Creative bulletin boards are a natural outgrowth of displaying students' written work along with the accompanying artwork. Use the IMAGINE THAT . . . headline as a 'header' to complete your bulletin board!

CONTENTS

IMAGINE THAT . . .

. . . You could invent a machine that could take you back in time!

THINK ABOUT/TALK ABOUT:

1. If you meet any two people who lived in the past, whom would you choose? Why?

2. Which era do you think would be the most exciting? Why?

3. Which era do you think would be the worst? Why?

4. If you could have lived in the past and been anything you wanted to be, something you can't be today, what would you have chosen to be? Why?

5. If you could send someone else back in time, who would you send and what time period would you choose? Why?

WRITE ABOUT . . .

WHAT'S A NICE KID LIKE ME DOING IN A TIME LIKE THIS?

You had your machine all ready to go back to the perfect time in history. But something went wrong—you pushed the wrong button, someone switched the time setting, a fuse blew out or something—and you have ended up in one of *these* times:

    A. Prehistoric times with the dinosaurs.
    B. In the middle of a Civil War battle.
    C. On a stagecoach being attacked by bandits.
    D. On a sailing ship being chased by pirates.
    E. On the Mayflower headed for the new world.

Tell how you got to the wrong place and time, how you felt about being there, what you did and saw, what happened to you, and how you got back to the present . . . if you did!

PICTURE THIS!

Draw a picture of the machine you invented to take you back in time or draw a picture of you when your machine took you to the wrong time and place.

IMAGINE THAT . . .

. . . All the televisions and video players in the world have disappeared and no one will ever be able to make another one!

THINK ABOUT/TALK ABOUT:

1. How would your life and that of your family be different if there were no TVs and video players?

2. What could you and your family do for entertainment without them?

3. Would there be any advantages to not having televisions and video players any more?

4. What are some of the good things about television that people would miss?

5. Do you think people watch too much television? Why? Do you watch too much TV?

WRITE ABOUT . . .

THE WAY IT USED TO BE WITH NO TV!

Find an older relative or neighbor you can interview who grew up without television. Here are some things you might want to ask:

    A. What did you do for entertainment?

    B. How were the radio story-programs then like the TV shows we watch today? How were they different?

    C. What did you think of TV when you first saw it?

    D. What do you think of the TV shows today?

    E. Do you think children watch too much TV today? Is it good or bad for them?

Ask a few questions of your own. Then write about what you think it would have been like growing up without television.

PICTURE THIS!

There are no more televisions and never will be. People need some kind of entertainment, though. Create a poster or drawing advertising what you think would be the best replacement . . . reading, model-making, indoor games, etc. but make it look and sound interesting!

IMAGINE THAT . . .
. . . Everyone in the world looked exactly alike!

THINK ABOUT/TALK ABOUT:

1. What would be some of the problems in a world where everyone looked alike?

2. Would there be any advantages about a world where everyone looked alike?

3. What do you imagine everyone would look like? Height, weight, build, hair, eyes, nose, smile, etc.

4. How would you like living in a world where all the people—even you—looked exactly the same?

5. Suppose everyone really looked alike. How do you think people could tell one another apart? What could they do to be different?

WRITE ABOUT . . .
EVERYONE I SEE . . . EXCEPT ME!

Suppose there was a world in which everyone looked exactly alike but for some reason you looked different. Tell your story. First describe what everyone else looks like and explain how you look different. Then tell how you feel about being different (weird, proud, special, ashamed???). Tell how people treat you. How does being the only different person in the world affect your life? What do you do about it?

PICTURE THIS!

If everyone on earth looked the same— only they didn't look like people as we know them—what would everyone look like? Draw a picture of what we would look like if we all looked alike but not human.

3.   Express Yourself! © THE MONKEY SISTERS, INC.

IMAGE THAT . . .

. . . You could change anything, but only ONE thing, about yourself!

THINK ABOUT/TALK ABOUT:

1. What are your best characteristics—things other people like most about you? . . . things you would never want to change? Name at least three. It might be interesting to ask friends or family about this!

2. If you could change one thing about your appearance, what would it be? Could such a change really be made?

3. If you could change one thing about your personality, what would it be? Why do you think this would make you a happier or better person? Could you make such a change if you really wanted to?

4. Some people judge others by the way they look. That's not a very good way to tell if someone is a good person or not. Discuss five characteristics of a good person that have nothing to do with appearance.

5. Everyone has good points and bad points. Almost everyone would like to change something about him/herself. Interview two adults you admire and can talk to easily. Ask each person what they like most and least about themselves.

WRITE ABOUT . . .

THE NEW YOU!

Write a description of the perfect you. What would you look like? How would you act? What kind of personality would you have? What could you do? How would others treat you? What kind of you would you be, if you could be perfect?

PICTURE THIS!

Draw a self-portrait of the new you . . . the perfect you, the way you would imagine yourself to be . . . or make a collage of cut-out magazine pictures to show what the new you would be like in terms of looks, clothes, actions and activities.

IMAGINE THAT . . .

. . . For some reason, you can only move and speak BACKWARDS!

THINK ABOUT/TALK ABOUT:

1. What kinds of problems would you run into if you could only *move* backwards?

2. What kinds of trouble might you get into if you could only *talk* backwards? (This could mean either your words come out backwards or everything you say comes out the opposite of what you mean—or both!)

3. How might other people react to your problem?

4. Have you ever said something that came out all wrong or got all jumbled up? How did you feel? Were you able to get your thoughts out straight eventually?

5. When a person has a handicap of some kind, he/she has to compensate and use other skills to make up for it. How could you compensate for only being able to move backwards? . . . talk backwards?

WRITE ABOUT . . .

!PLEH

Write a story about the day you could only move and speak backwards. How did you first discover you had this unusual condition? What do you think caused it? What problems did it create—serious or funny? How did you make it through the day? Were your friends helpful or did they make the problem worse for you? How was your condition cured?

PICTURE THIS!

Write a message to a friend, but write the message backwards in "mirror writing." (You'll know you've gotten it right when you can hold your message up to a mirror and read it correctly.) . . . or try to draw something, a face, a building, an object of some sort that looks exactly the same upside down as it does right side up.

Express Yourself! © THE MONKEY SISTERS, INC.

IMAGINE THAT . . .

. . . You are the parent and your parent is the child!

THINK ABOUT/TALK ABOUT:

1. What are the advantages of being the child? The disadvantages?

2. What are the advantages of being the parent? The disadvantages?

3. If you were the parent and your parent was your child, what would you do the same way your parent does it now?

4. If you were the parent and your parent was your child, what would you do differently?

5. Would you make a good parent? Why?

WRITE ABOUT . . .

THAT'S MY KID!

Suppose you are the parent and your parent (only one of them) is your child. How would you describe your child to someone else? Try to imagine your parent as a child your age. Describe what your child looks like, acts like, good points and bad points, the things you're proud of and the things that drive you crazy. Just what kind of child would you imagine your parent to be?

PICTURE THIS!

Draw a picture of you and a favorite adult doing something together. It could be some activity you really do enjoy together, or something you would like to do with this parent, friend, relative or neighbor you like.

IMAGINE THAT . . .

. . . You could have dinner tonight with anyone in the world!

THINK ABOUT/TALK ABOUT:

1. If you could have dinner with anyone, whom would you choose? Why?

2. Where would you go for dinner? What kind of restaurant do you think this person would like? Or would you invite this person to your home for dinner?

3. If it was up to you to pick the menu for your special guest, what would you have? What do you think he/she would like? Tell what you would choose for the main course, dessert, etc.

4. What do you think your guest would wear to dinner? What would *you* wear?

5. What would you talk about at dinner? Do you think this person would be easy to talk to? Why?

WRITE ABOUT . . .

I'VE ALWAYS WANTED TO ASK YOU!

If you did have dinner with someone famous or important or special in some way, you would want to have something to talk about. Make a list of ten questions you would ask. Try to make the questions ones that would encourage your guest to talk to you, not just say "yes" or "no."

PICTURE THIS!

Draw or cut out magazine pictures of the outfit you would wear to this special dinner.

IMAGINE THAT . . .

. . . You've just won a big contest, and your prize is a trip anywhere in the world!

THINK ABOUT/TALK ABOUT:

1. If you could go anywhere in the world, where would you go? Why?

2. What makes this place different from where you live?

3. What one place in the world would you least like to go? Why?

4. If you were going on your prize trip to the place of your dreams, what special things would you have to pack to take with you?

5. What was the best trip you've ever taken? Why?

WRITE ABOUT . . .

WISH YOU WERE HERE!

Take a sheet of art paper and divide one side into two sections to look like the back of a postcard. On the "message" side, write to a relative or friend about the wonderful prize trip you're taking. Tell something of what you've seen and done on the trip, something that's been especially exciting, interesting or just plain fun. Don't forget to address the card and put a "stamp" (draw one) in the corner.

PICTURE THIS!

On the other side of the postcard, draw a scene from the dream trip you've won . . . a picture of something you would actually be able to see if you really did take a trip to the place you would most like to visit.

IMAGINE THAT . . .

. . . You can be your favorite television character for just one day!

THINK ABOUT/TALK ABOUT:

1. Who is your favorite character on television?

2. What do you especially like about this character? What makes him/her/it so special? Does the character have any faults?

3. What do you like about the life this character leads in his television role? What kinds of things does the character do that you would like to do?

4. How are you and this character alike? Different?

5. Is this character realistic? Does he/she/it seem like real people you know? Is he/she/it smarter, braver, better than most people are?

WRITE ABOUT . . .

WHAT WOULD I DO IF I WERE YOU?

Write a letter to your favorite character on television. In the first paragraph, tell the character why you would like to be him/her/it for a day. Then, in the rest of the letter, tell the character what you would do during your day in his/her place. Where would you go? Whom would you want to meet (the other characters on the show)? Would you do things the same or differently than the character does?

PICTURE THIS!

Make a poster advertising your favorite television show. Be sure your poster illustrates something special about the show—what makes it so funny or exciting or mysterious or unusual. Add a clever slogan that might interest other people in watching it, especially people who have never seen the show before.

IMAGINE THAT . . .

. . . You have the power to uninvent one modern-day invention!

THINK ABOUT/TALK ABOUT:

1. What do you think are the five most important and useful inventions in today's world?

2. What do you think are the two worst inventions ever made? What is bad about each one?

3. If you uninvent any one machine, which would you choose?

4. How would the world be better without that invention?

5. How do you think most other people would react to your uninvention? Would they miss the machine? Would they be pleased or angry with you?

WRITE ABOUT . . .

A WORLD WITHOUT !

Decide which one invention most deserves to be uninvented. Fill in the name of that invention/machine in the title of your essay. Describe what the world would be like if you really could get rid of the machine. Tell both the good things and the problems, if any, in a world without this invention. Think about how your decision to uninvent this machine would affect other people and their lives.

PICTURE THIS!

Since you've just uninvented something, it's up to you to invent a substitute. For example, if you've uninvented cars, you need to invent a better means of transportation. Draw a picture of the invention you've come up with to replace the one you uninvented. Give your new invention a good name, tell what it does and explain why it's better than the machine you did away with.

IMAGINE THAT . . .

. . . You are a runner, running second, in a marathon race in the Olympics!

THINK ABOUT/TALK ABOUT:

1. What would be the difficulties of running a marathon race?

2. How would you feel about being second?

3. How would you feel about the person running ahead of you?

4. How would you feel if you finished second? How might your family feel?

5. What would make the Olympic race different than any other race you might enter?

WRITE ABOUT . . .

THE SECOND PLACE RACE!

You've tried your best. You've won the silver medal, coming in second in the long, hard marathon race. You're standing there now, with the silver medal around your neck, as the anthem for the first place runner's country is played. Write down what goes through your mind as you stand there on the platform. How do you feel about your effort in the race? What makes you feel proud? What makes you sad? How do you feel about the medal you've won? Do you think your teammates and family will be proud or disappointed? How do you feel about the person who came in only a few seconds ahead of you? Was it worth all the training and hard work you went through? Will you try again in the next Olympics?

PICTURE THIS!

All of us have special talents. Unfortunately, we can't usually earn gold or silver medals for things like being a good friend, reading lots of books, being a computer whiz, playing the piano, etc. If you COULD win a medal for your special talent, what would it look like? What would it say? What would that talent be? Design the medal you could win for something you are—or something you can do.

IMAGINE THAT . . .

. . . You are a double-dip ice cream cone on a hot summer afternoon!

THINK ABOUT/TALK ABOUT:

1. What two flavors would you choose to be?

2. What kind of personality would an ice cream cone have? Would the two flavors have different personalities? Would they get along?

3. How would you feel about the hot summer afternoon?

4. What kind of person has just bought you?

5. How would that person feel about you on that hot afternoon?

WRITE ABOUT . . .

DRIP! DRIP! DOUBLE-DIP!

Write a dialogue between the two scoops of ice cream as they're dipped onto a cone and handed over to a customer on a hot summer afternoon. Give each dip a name that suits the flavor. The conversation can be funny or serious. The two dips can be great friends or not get along at all on top of that cone!

When you're all finished act out the conversation with a classmate. You may want to act out your scene in front of the class to see who comes up with the cleverest double-dip script!

PICTURE THIS!

Divide your drawing paper into three equal parts. Draw yourself as a double-dip cone that is (1) freshly dipped (2) partly eaten, and (3) nearly finished. Think about how your expression would change at each stage of your life as a double-dip cone.

IMAGINE THAT...

...The entire water supply in your area has suddenly turned into cherry soda!

THINK ABOUT/TALK ABOUT:

1. How do you think the children in your area might react?

2. How do you think the adults in your area might react?

3. What might be some funny problems caused by a cherry soda water supply?

4. What might be some of the serious problems caused by a cherry soda water supply?

5. What could a community do about a cherry soda water supply?

WRITE ABOUT...

THE PINK DRINK IN MY SINK!

Write a story about the time your area's water supply turned to cherry soda. Tell how people reacted when they first found out about the problem. Describe some of the good things and bad things (the pros and cons) about a cherry soda water supply. Tell how the problem affected you and your family. See if you can come up with a really unique way to solve the problem at the end of your story.

PICTURE THIS!

Draw a picture illustrating one of the problems (serious or funny) of a cherry soda water supply.

IMAGINE THAT . . .

. . . Every time somebody says your name out loud, you suddenly and mysteriously turn into a big, hairy monster and you stay that way for the next 15 minutes!

THINK ABOUT/TALK ABOUT:

1. Who are some of the people who usually say your name during the day?

2. How might these people react to your sudden change in appearance?

3. If you did turn into a big, hairy monster, what kind of personality do you think you'd have?

4. Would you enjoy the change, or would you try to keep people from saying your name? Why?

5. How could you solve such a problem?

WRITE ABOUT . . .

A MONSTROUS EXPERIENCE!

Tell what happened the day when every time someone said your name you turned into a hairy monster for fifteen minutes. How did it start? Where and when did people say your name? How did you feel? How did others react? What did you do while you were a monster? Were your experiences funny or scary? How did you solve the monstrous problem?

PICTURE THIS!

Draw a picture of the hairy monster you turned into when somebody said your name.

IMAGINE THAT . . .

. . . You have to spend the next twenty-four hours as an insect!

THINK ABOUT/TALK ABOUT:

1. What kind of insect would you choose to be? Why?

2. What would be the advantages of being a bug?

3. What kinds of worries and problems would a bug have to face?

4. How would your life be different than that of a human being?

5. Would you be glad or sad when the twenty-four hours were over? Why?

WRITE ABOUT . . .

DON'T BUG ME!

Write about the day you spent as an insect. What kind of bug were you? Were you a helpful insect or a harmful one? What did you look like? How did you feel? What did you do in the course of the day? Did you have a name? Did you have any adventures with some buggy friends? Did you run into any humans during the day? If so, how did they act when they saw you?

PICTURE THIS!

Draw a picture of yourself as an insect. Try to give your bug-portrait some of the characteristics of both the insect and your real, human personality . . . try to show what *you* would really look like as a bug!

Express Yourself! © THE MONKEY SISTERS, INC.

IMAGINE THAT . . .

. . . When you woke up this morning you discovered that you were invisible!

THINK ABOUT/TALK ABOUT:

1. How did you feel when you discovered you were invisible? Happy, frightened, excited, or sad?

2. What would your family say and do?

3. What would happen if you went to school that way?

4. What would be some of the problems of being invisible?

5. How could you put your invisibility to good use?

WRITE ABOUT . . .

NOW YOU SEE ME, NOW YOU DON'T!

Write a story about the day you were invisible. How did you discover your unusual condition? How did you feel about it? How did you break the news to your family? What did they say and do? Where did you go and what did you do while nobody could see you? Did you get into any trouble? Did you have any fun? Did you use your invisibility to play tricks on people, or to help someone? Did you stay invisible . . . or did you manage to find an unusual solution to such an uncommon problem?

PICTURE THIS!

You can't really draw a picture of yourself if you were invisible . . . BUT, you could draw a picture of your family, and the expressions on their faces, when they saw . . . or rather *didn't* see you . . . OR, you could draw a picture of something you did while nobody could see you!

IMAGINE THAT . . .

. . . You have a very bad case of the hiccups— and every time you "hic" you grow two inches taller!

THINK ABOUT/TALK ABOUT:

1. Would you want to be taller than you are or not? Why?

2. What kind of trouble—funny or serious—might such a quick and steady change of height cause for you and those around you?

3. What could your friends and family do to try to cure your hiccups?

4. At what point would your new height begin to cause you problems?

5. Would you be able to get back to your normal size again? Would you want to?

WRITE ABOUT . . .

A SMALL, TALL TALE

Tell the story of the day you had the hiccups that made you grow . . . and grow . . . and grow. How and when and where did you first notice that you were growing? How did you feel about it? What did those who saw you do and say? What problems did your new height cause you? How did others try to help you? Did it work? How were your hiccups cured? Were you able to get back to your normal height again?

PICTURE THIS!

Draw a picture of a scene from your small, tall tale. Pick the funniest or most horrible thing that happened to you the day you hiccuped yourself into a very BIG problem.

17.   Express Yourself! © THE MONKEY SISTERS, INC.

IMAGINE THAT . . .

. . . You are a big dill pickle in a jar on your supermarket shelf!

THINK ABOUT/TALK ABOUT:

1. What kind of personality would a dill pickle have?

2. How would you feel about being stuck in that jar with all those other pickles?

3. What would you and the other pickles find to talk about?

4. What kind of customers would you see walking by?

5. Would you want someone to buy you or not? Why?

WRITE ABOUT . . .

A SOUR NOTE!

You are a dill pickle in a jar full of other pickles on the pickle shelf at your local supermarket. Write a letter to your family back at the cucumber farm. Tell them how you like your life as a pickle in a pickle jar. Tell them about your pickle-mates, why you like them or not, how you get along, what you do to pass the time as you wait on the shelf. You might include a funny story or two . . . something you saw happen in the grocery store, some funny customers you saw. Be sure to sign your letter with a good pickle name!

PICTURE THIS!

Imagine that you and some of your friends or family members are pickles in a jar. Draw a picture of you and your pickle-mates. Be sure to give each pickle a personality, some individual expressions and features, and a good pickle name.

IMAGINE THAT . . .

. . . Everybody you meet will do exactly what you tell them to do for the next twenty-four hours!

THINK ABOUT/TALK ABOUT:

1. How would you feel having that kind of power over other people?

2. Who would you most like to have in your power for twenty-four hours?

3. What would you ask that person to do while he/she was in your power?

4. What might be some ways to put such a power to good use?

5. What might be some uses for such a power that might not be so good?

WRITE ABOUT . . .

THE "DO-AS-I-SAY" DAY!

Write about the day when you could make anybody do anything you wanted them to do. On whom did you use the power? What did you make them do? How did they feel about obeying your commands? Did you use your power for good or evil purposes? How did you feel about having such a power? Were you sorry to lose it when the day was over? What happened when the power was gone . . . did anyone try to get even? What would you do with a "do-as-I-say" day?

PICTURE THIS!

Illustrate a scene from your story, showing someone under your power doing something you asked him/her to do.

IMAGINE THAT . . .

. . . This morning, in the middle of phys ed class, you accidentally discovered that you could fly!

THINK ABOUT/TALK ABOUT:

1. What were you doing at the time you accidentally discovered you could fly?

2. What did your phys ed teacher do and say?

3. How did you feel about flying once you tried it?

4. Would it be a blessing or a curse to be able to fly? Why?

5. If you really could fly, where would you go?

WRITE ABOUT . . .

HIGH THERE!

Write about your rather unusual phys ed class this morning when you accidentally discovered you were able to fly. Tell how you discovered your talent. Tell what your teacher and classmates said and did when they saw you. Tell how you felt about it. Where did you go in the school? What kind of reaction did you get from the other students and teachers, the principal, the custodians? Did anything exciting or funny happen? How did you lose or use your new talent?

PICTURE THIS!

Draw a picture of your phys ed class at the moment you first found out that you could fly.

IMAGINE THAT . . .

. . . Your favorite cartoon character has come to life and is standing at your front door!

THINK ABOUT/TALK ABOUT:

1. Which cartoon character is your favorite? Why?

2. How would you feel if you opened your front door and found this character standing there . . . alive?

3. How would your family feel if you invited this character in for dinner?

4. What would you and the character find to talk about?

5. What one thing would you ask this character to do for you if he/she really showed up at your door?

WRITE ABOUT . . .

GUESS WHO!

Write about your adventure with your favorite cartoon character. What happened when you brought the character in to meet the family? What happened when you took him/her to school? Did you have any exciting or funny adventures together? Did you do something heroic or did you get into mischief together? Were you sorry to see the character go when the visit was over?

PICTURE THIS!

Draw a picture of you and your favorite cartoon character sharing an adventure . . . serious or funny . . . together.

IMAGINE THAT . . .

. . . You just found an old chest with a million dollars inside!

THINK ABOUT/TALK ABOUT:

1. Where might the money have come from? Give two or three possibilities.

2. What would you do with the money?

3. If you decided to spend it, what would be the first three things you would buy?

4. If you decided to use the money for good deeds, what would be the first good deed you would do?

5. How do you think people would treat you when they found out you had so much money?

WRITE ABOUT . . .

STASH THE CASH!

On your way to school this morning, you found an old chest with a million dollars inside. You need to stash the cash someplace . . . inside your school . . . till you can decide what to do with it. You don't want to tell anybody where the money is hidden, but you're willing to give some clues. Think of a good place to stash the cash. Then write five good, tricky clues about where the money is hidden. Give some information in each clue, but try not to give too much. Exchange your list of clues with one of your classmates. Did you figure out where your classmate stashed the cash or did you have to be told?

PICTURE THIS!

Draw a map that leads from this classroom to the cash that you've stashed somewhere else in the school. Make your treasure map as clear and exact as you can—good enough so that somebody could really follow it if they had to.

IMAGINE THAT . . .

. . . You are the wastepaper basket in this classroom!

THINK ABOUT/TALK ABOUT:

1. List ten words that describe yourself.

2. What kind of personality do you think a wastepaper basket might have?

3. How would you feel about all the things that are thrown into you all day? What are some of the good things? What are some of the worst?

4. What are some of the unusual or funny sights and sounds you see from your post in this classroom?

5. Is this classroom a good or bad home for a wastepaper basket like you? Why?

WRITE ABOUT . . .

A CAN'S DEMANDS!

You are a trash can in this room. You are sick and tired of the way you're being treated! You are going to go on strike unless people stop treating you like garbage! Make a list of ten demands—ten rules you'd like people in this class to start following to treat you more fairly and make your life as the classroom wastepaper basket a little easier.

PICTURE THIS!

Draw a picture of a protest march of garbage, trash, and wastepaper cans marching in a row, carrying picket signs to let people know their complaints and feelings. Be sure to have catchy sayings on the signs, too!

Express Yourself! © THE MONKEY SISTERS, INC.

IMAGINE THAT . . .

. . . You have just turned into a serving of your all-time favorite food!

THINK ABOUT/TALK ABOUT:

1. What is your favorite food? Why?

2. Describe yourself as your favorite food. What would you look like, smell like, feel like, taste like?

3. What would be the complications of being a walking, talking serving of whatever food you like the best?

4. What would your family say and do when they saw what had happened to you?

5. Would you ever be able to turn back to yourself again? If so, how? If not, what would happen to you?

WRITE ABOUT . . .

THE INCREDIBLE, EDIBLE ME!

You have just looked into the mirror and have you been surprised! You finally ate so much that you turned into some. Tell what happens during your day as a serving of your favorite food, from the time you look into that mirror until the time you go to bed as yourself again (or are gobbled up, or whatever). What problems do you have? How do people react to your condition? Are you in any danger of being eaten? Do you solve the problem or do you stay a serving of food forever?

PICTURE THIS!

Draw a big square. Pretend that's the mirror you looked into this morning. Inside the square, in the "mirror" you've drawn, draw a picture of what you saw—a picture of yourself as your favorite food!

IMAGINE THAT . . .

. . . You have suddenly become the smartest person in the world!

THINK ABOUT/TALK ABOUT:

1. Would you be pleased or upset to find out you had suddenly become so smart?

2. How would being the smartest person in the world change your life?

3. What might be the disadvantages of being so smart?

4. How could you put your super-intelligence to work to help mankind?

5. Would people treat you any differently once they found out how smart you had become? Why?

WRITE ABOUT . . .

THE MAIN BRAIN!

As the smartest person in the world, you have been called upon by the president to invent three brand new, much-needed inventions that will probably change the world. Tell what three new, important inventions you invented. Describe what each one looks like and the job it does. Use your super-brain to come up with a good name for each invention, too.

PICTURE THIS!

Draw a picture of your latest super-brain invention . . . THE NEVER FAIL, ALWAYS RIGHT, SUPER-DUPER HOMEWORK MACHINE! Guaranteed to do any and all homework in thirty seconds and never make mistakes! Use your imagination to design the perfect (funny or serious) homework machine.

IMAGINE THAT . . .

. . . You are a wad of bubble gum!

THINK ABOUT/TALK ABOUT:

1. What flavor gum would you choose? Why?

2. If you were a wad of bubble gum, where might you find yourself?

3. What would be the worst things about being a wad of gum?

4. What ways do you think a wad of gum might prove itself helpful and useful?

5. Would a wad of gum have enemies? If so, who might they be?

WRITE ABOUT . . .

CHEW CHEW TRAINING!

You are a young stick of bubble gum, just starting bubble gum training. What kinds of skills would they teach you in the Bubble Gum Academy? What kinds of courses would you have to take? What kinds of dangers would they warn you to look out for? How would you know you were ready to "graduate" to a pack of gum and go out and make your way in the world? Tell all about your chew-chew training at bubble gum school!

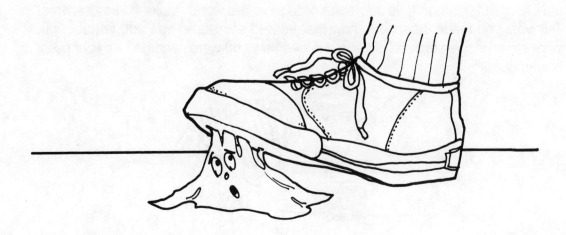

PICTURE THIS!

Draw a picture of yourself as a wad of gum. Give yourself an appropriate bubble-gum name.

IMAGINE THAT . . .

. . . You are a magician who can make anything disappear—the only problem is you just can't bring it back again!

THINK ABOUT/TALK ABOUT:

1. What five things would you most like to make disappear?
   (Remember, you can't bring them back!)

2. What good uses can you think of for such a power?

3. How might other people try to get you to use your power?

4. What do you think would happen to all the things you make disappear? Where would they go?

5. Would you really like to be a magician? Why?

WRITE ABOUT . . .

NOW YOU SEE IT, NOW YOU DON'T!

You are a rather unusual magician. You have the power to make anything disappear . . . forever. In fact, once you make something disappear, you can't bring it back again. Tell about the time you used your power to do something really useful for mankind, to help someone or to save the world. Make yourself a hero! Tell what you made disappear, how that helped someone, how you felt about it, what other people said and did about it, and how you were rewarded for your great heroic deed.

PICTURE THIS!

Divide a piece of paper into eight squares. In each square, draw something (or someone) you wouldn't mind making disappear.

IMAGINE THAT . . .

. . . You are a caveman who has been frozen in time and you've just come back to life in today's modern world!

THINK ABOUT/TALK ABOUT:

1. Everything is different today than it was when you were frozen . . . the animals, people's looks and clothing, our modern machines, our houses and cities . . . How would you feel when you woke up and saw all these strange and wonderful things?

2. What might frighten you about the new world?

3. How do you think people would treat you when they saw you?

4. What kind of problems would you have communicating? How could you "talk" to the people you meet?

5. What kinds of things would you need to learn to survive in the new world?

WRITE ABOUT . . .

CAVE SWEET CAVE

Imagine that you are a caveman who is just spending his first night in a modern-day house. Tell how you feel. Describe some of the weird and wonderful things you see. What do you think these things are for? (Remember, you've never seen things like a washing machine, a television, or a bathtub before!) Does anything surprise or frighten you? What do you especially like? Dislike? Does anything strange or funny happen while you're trying out some of the modern-day inventions? How do you like your modern-day cave?

PICTURE THIS!

Draw a picture ot yourself as a caveman/woman using some modern-day invention you've never seen before.

IMAGINE THAT . . .

. . . You are a broken toy that nobody plays with anymore?

THINK ABOUT/TALK ABOUT:

1. What kind of toy would you be? Why?

2. How did you get broken? What's the matter with you?

3. How do you feel about not being used anymore?

4. If you were fixed, what kind of child would you like to have find you and play with you?

5. Of all the toys you've ever had, what was your favorite, and why?

WRITE ABOUT . . .

THE NO-JOY TOY!

Here are the first two lines of a poem about a broken toy that nobody plays with anymore. Finish the toy's poem. You can make it as long as you wish, but be sure to add at least four more lines.

Here I sit upon the shelf,
Feeling sorry for myself—

(the rest is up to you!)

PICTURE THIS!

Draw a picture of yourself as a broken toy nobody plays with anymore.

IMAGINE THAT . . .

. . . You are a bright, red helium balloon in the hands of a three-year-old child!

THINK ABOUT/TALK ABOUT:

1. How would the child feel to have you?

2. How and where do you think the child might have gotten you?

3. What would be the dangers of being a helium balloon in the hands of a three-year-old child?

4. Would you want to stay with the child or float away? Why?

5. How would the child feel if you escaped?

WRITE ABOUT . . .

UP, UP AND AWAY!

OOPS! The child has let go of you after all! You're free! Write about your adventures as a free-floating, bright red helium balloon. How did you feel when you were let go? How did you feel as you rose into the sky? What kind of view did you have? What did you see? Where did you go? Did you like traveling around that way? Were there any dangers? Where did you end up? What happened the day you went, up, up and away?

PICTURE THIS!

Draw a picture of yourself as a bright red helium balloon floating over your house, or your school, or some special place in the town where you live.

IMAGINE THAT...

... You and your friends were making fudge when you noticed that the fudge was rising out of the pot, over the stove and filling up the kitchen ... and you just couldn't get the fudge to stop oozing!

THINK ABOUT/TALK ABOUT:

1. What kind of fudge would you be making?

2. What would you and your friends do when they first notice the fudge is out of control?

3. What would be the pros and cons about having so much fudge?

4. What ways could you try to keep the fudge from growing? Would any of them work?

5. If you don't get the fudge to stop oozing and growing, what do you think might happen?

WRITE ABOUT...

SWEET TO EAT, BUT NOT TOO NEAT!

Write about the day the fudge took over your house ... or your town ... or the world! Tell how the whole, sticky mess started. Tell what happened, what people did, what problems arose as the fudge oozed out of control. Tell how you tried to control the fudge and how you finally got it to stop ... IF YOU DID! And, if it did stop, just how would you get rid of all that candy?

PICTURE THIS!

Draw a picture of the fudge as it oozed out of control in your kitchen or as it threatened to take over your house.

IMAGINE THAT . . .

. . . You are the world's only talking skunk!

THINK ABOUT/TALK ABOUT:

1. What would be good about being a skunk?

2. What would be bad about your skunky life?

3. How would people react when they saw you?

4. How would they react when they found out you could talk?

5. What's the number one thing you'd like to tell people about skunks and the way they're treated?

WRITE ABOUT . . .

SMELLY ON THE TELLY!

You are a television reporter about to interview the world's only talking skunk. Make up six good questions you might want to ask him. Then write down the answers you think a talking skunk would give. Here's an example: (But don't use these!)

REPORTER: How do you stand that smell, Mr. Stinker?

SKUNK: What smell?

PICTURE THIS!

Make a mini-poster advertising an appearance in your school auditorium by the world's only talking skunk. Make the program sound really interesting! Give the talking skunk a catchy name, too! And, don't forget a good title for the program you're advertising!

IMAGINE THAT . . .

. . . You took a hot bath this morning, and it must have been way too hot because you seem to have shrunk and now you're only six inches tall!

THINK ABOUT/TALK ABOUT:

1. What problems might a six-inch tall person run into?

2. How did you even manage to get out of the bathtub?

3. Would there be any advantages to being so small?

4. How did the people you know react when they saw you?

5. How could you go about getting yourself to grow again?

WRITE ABOUT . . .

A VERY SMALL PROBLEM!

Here are some "small" problems a six-inch person might have. Tell why each would be a major problem for such a small person. Then tell how you would solve each problem if you were only six inches tall.

- getting dressed
- brushing your teeth
- eating a hot dog
- riding a schoolbus
- crossing a street
- being in class
- writing a paper
- walking your dog
- swatting a fly
- finding a job

PICTURE THIS!

Illustrate one of the problems you ran into when you were only six inches tall. Draw a picture.

IMAGINE THAT . . .

. . . You are in the washroom at school. When you look into the mirror to check your hair, you discover that you've turned GREEN!

THINK ABOUT/TALK ABOUT:

1. What would your immediate reaction be? How would you feel? What would you do?

2. What would be the reaction when you return to your classroom?

3. How might you have turned green in the first place? What might have caused such a change?

4. How would people treat you if you were green?

5. Would there be any advantage to being green?

WRITE ABOUT . . .
A COLORFUL EXPERIENCE
Tell what happened the day you turned green. Start from when you looked into that restroom mirror. Show what your colorful day was like and how you managed to get yourself back to normal again (if you ever did!).

PICTURE THIS!
Draw JUST THE FACES (to show expressions) of the following people the first time they saw that you were green: yourself, your teacher, your parents, your best friend, your worst enemy.

IMAGINE THAT . . .

. . . You are a world famous race car driver in the middle of a championship race!

THINK ABOUT/TALK ABOUT:

1. What would be some of the things you might be thinking about as you drive your car?

2. What would be the dangers of your job?

3. Would you be leading the race, or trying to catch up with the leader?

4. How do you feel about being a famous race car driver? Why?

5. How would you feel if you won the race? How would you feel if you lost?

WRITE ABOUT . . .

THE CAR STAR!

You are a world-famous race car driver who has just won a big, championship race. A newspaper reporter is interviewing you for an article in the paper. Here are the questions she asks you. You have to supply the answers.

1. How long have you been a race car driver?
2. What made you decide to go into racing?
3. What do you like most about racing?
4. What don't you like about your career?
5. What are your biggest worries during a race?
6. How does your family feel about you being a race car driver?
7. How does it feel to be famous?
8. What will you do when you retire from racing?
9. How will you spend all the money you've just won?
10. What would you have done if you had lost the race?

PICTURE THIS!

Draw a picture of your race car and you after you've won.

IMAGINE THAT . . .

. . . The principal has just put YOU in charge of this class for the day!

THINK ABOUT/TALK ABOUT:

1. Would this be a good class to take charge of? Why or why not?

2. What kind of problems might you have if you really were in charge of the class for the day?

3. How would your classmates react to having you in charge?

4. Would you make a good teacher? Why or why not?

5. Would you be glad or sad when your day-in-charge was over? Why?

WRITE ABOUT . . .

NOW HEAR THIS!

You are in charge of this class for the day! It's up to you to make the rules you expect the class to follow. Make a list of ten 'Rules of the Day.' You might want to make your list 10 serious rules that every good class should follow. Or, for fun, you might want to make up a list of 10 silly rules . . . rules that might make for a very interesting class indeed!

PICTURE THIS!

Draw a picture of yourself as the substitute teacher for this class.

IMAGINE THAT . . .

. . . You are an alligator living in a swamp!

THINK ABOUT/TALK ABOUT:

1. What would be a good name for a swamp alligator?

2. What kind of personality would a swamp alligator have?

3. How would a swamp alligator spend its day?

4. What would be the pros and cons of being an alligator in a swamp?

5. How would the other swamp creatures treat you? Why?

WRITE ABOUT . . .

SEE YOU LATER. ALLIGATOR!

You've been a swamp alligator for years . . . and are bored. You're really tired of that old swamp, so you decide to go somewhere else for a little excitement and adventure. Suppose you show up in this town or city—maybe at this school. Tell about your adventure. What would you see and do that would be new and exciting or even funny or scary to an alligator? How would the people in this town react to an unexpected visit from an alligator? Would you stay or would you be glad to go back to your swamp again?

PICTURE THIS!

Illustrate a scene from your story—the day you, the alligator, showed up in this town!

IMAGINE THAT . . .

. . . You are a parachutist standing at the open door of the airplane just about to make your very first jump!

THINK ABOUT/TALK ABOUT:

1. How would you feel standing there, looking out into space, knowing you are about to jump?

2. Describe the view you have from the door of the plane.

3. How would it feel gliding down through space?

4. Why might you be jumping in the first place . . . for fun, as part of your job? If it's part of your job, what kind of work do you do?

5. How would your family feel about you making the jump?

WRITE ABOUT . . .

IT'S A LONG WAY DOWN!

Describe your first parachute jump. Start as you step up to the open door of the plane. Tell how you feel as you look out . . . how it feels to stand there with the 'chute on your back. Describe what you feel and see and do as you jump from the plane and as you float down through the sky. How does it feel when your 'chute opens? Describe your landing. How do you feel after your first jump is over? Would you do it again?

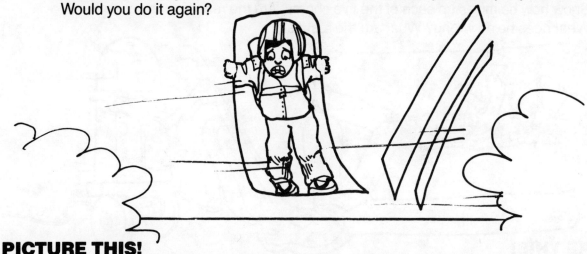

PICTURE THIS!

Draw a picture of your school and the area around it . . . as you would see it if you were really a parachutist floating down toward the school.

IMAGINE THAT . . .

. . . For your birthday you have been given a robot that you can program to do any five chores you choose!

THINK ABOUT/TALK ABOUT :

1. Think about all the things you have to do each day . . . at school, at home, etc. Which five things that you have to do on a regular basis would you want your new robot to do for you?

2. How would your friends feel about you having a robot to do your work for you?

3. What would your parents and teachers think of you having a robot to do your work for you?

4. Would there be any disadvantages in having a robot do your chores?

5. What would be a good name for such a robot?

WRITE ABOUT . . .

THE MIXED-UP MECHANICAL MAN!

For your birthday, you have been given a robot that will do any five chores for you. You've already programmed the robot to do the five chores you least like to do yourself. Unfortunately, when you turn on your mechanical man, you discover he's a little mixed up. He gets things sort of backwards and nothing he does turns out quite right. Tell what happens when you turn on your mixed-up mechanical man. Show how he mixes up each of the five chores. Are the results funny or serious? What does he do wrong? What are the results?

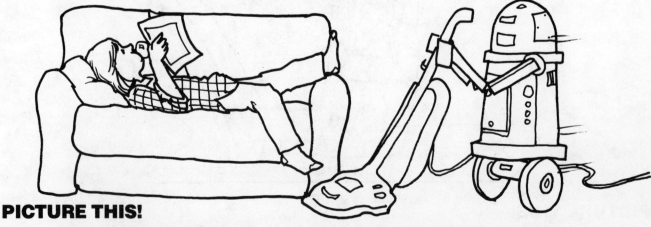

PICTURE THIS!

Draw a picture of your mixed-up mechanical birthday robot doing one of the chores you programmed him to do.

IMAGINE THAT . . .

. . . You are a marshall in the old, wild west!

THINK ABOUT/TALK ABOUT:

1. How would life be different in those days than it is now?

2. How would a law officer's job have been different then than it is now?

3. What kind of problems and outlaws would you have to take care of?

4. What would you like about your job?

5. Would you really like to be a law officer? Why?

WRITE ABOUT . . .

REACH FOR THE SKY!

Tell how you solved your biggest case as a wild west, old time marshall. Did you capture a train robber, a bank robber, or a cattle rustler . . . single-handedly bring in a famous outlaw gang . . . have a shoot-out with some mean and nasty gunslinger? Tell what happened the day you were a marshall in the old, wild west.

PICTURE THIS!

Draw a 'WANTED' poster for the outlaw/s you captured in the big adventure you just wrote about. Tell what his name or the name of the gang is. Tell how much reward was offered and what the outlaw/s were wanted for.

IMAGINE THAT . . .

. . . When you got to school this morning there was already someone sitting at your desk— someone who looks exactly like you!

THINK ABOUT/TALK ABOUT:

1. What would be your first reaction to finding a double sitting at your desk?

2. What would your teacher and classmates do and say when they found out there were two of you?

3. What kind of problems might having a double cause you?

4. What kind of fun might you have if you really had a double?

5. Would you take the double home to meet your family? Why?

WRITE ABOUT . . .

DOUBLE TROULE!

The trouble with your double is that everyone thinks the double is the real you, and you are the impostor. You have to prove, beyond a doubt, that you are really who you claim to be. Your teacher has given you the chance to prove your identity by telling your classmates ten things about yourself, things that are unique about you—things your classmates would recognize or remember. You have to find things that make you really different and special . . . things only you have or do or say—traits and habits and talents that are yours alone!

PICTURE THIS!

Draw a picture of your double sitting at your desk. (Of course, it could just as easily be a picture of you, too!)

IMAGINE THAT . . .

. . . You have the power to make it rain or snow whenever you want and as much as you want!

THINK ABOUT/TALK ABOUT:

1. What would be some of the good things you could do with such a power? How could you use it to help others?

2. How might an evil person use such a power? What bad ways might he/she put such a power to use?

3. How do you feel about rainy days? Why?

4. What problems might you cause if you made it snow twelve inches in a place where it doesn't usually snow at all?

5. Would you like it to snow twelve inches tonight where you live? Why?

WRITE ABOUT . . .

RAIN, RAIN GO AWAY!

It's raining. It's been raining for two weeks! It's beginning to look like it will never stop raining. Write a story about the rain that wouldn't go away. Tell how you feel about the rain. Tell how all the rain is affecting people's spirits and tempers. Tell the problems and dangers the endless rain is causing. Tell how it affects your life and the life of others in your town. What can you do about so much rain?

PICTURE THIS!

Which do you like better, rain or snow? Draw either a 'rain picture' (something you like to do in the rain) or a 'snow picture' (something you like to do in the snow).

IMAGINE THAT . . .

. . . No matter what anyone says to you, for the next 24 hours all you can do is laugh!

THINK ABOUT/TALK ABOUT:

1. How would you feel if a friend laughed at everything you said?

2. How would you feel if you couldn't control your laughter, if no matter how hard you tried, you laughed at everything you heard?

3. How might your friends, teachers, and/or family react to your sudden uncontrollable case of giggles?

4. What kind of trouble might you get into in the course of a day?

5. What might be a good cure for an uncontrollable case of laughter?

WRITE ABOUT . . .

NO LAUGHING MATTER!

Write about the day you started laughing and you just couldn't stop. No matter what happened, no matter what anyone said or did, you only laughed harder and louder. Tell how this unusual problem might have started, what kind of problems it caused you, how other people reacted to your unusual condition, what you and others did to cure the laughs, and how the whole problem ended.

PICTURE THIS!

Draw something that's supposed to make people laugh . . . a cartoon. It can be your own version of a cartoon or comic strip you enjoy or you can make up a new one based on something at home, at school, in the news or whatever your imagination suggests.

IMAGINE THAT . . .

. . . You are an animal in the zoo!

THINK ABOUT/TALK ABOUT:

1. What kind of zoo animal would you most like to be?

2. What kind of zoo animal would you least like to be?

3. What would be the advantage of living in a zoo?

4. Would you rather be living in the wild? Why?

5. What do you think of all the people who come to the zoo to look at you?

WRITE ABOUT . . .

NEW IN THE ZOO!

You are the newest animal in the zoo. Thousands of people are here to see you because you are so unusual. You see, there has never been an animal quite like you before, *EVER!* You are entirely new! You look like a combination of five different animals and you have some very unusual habits too!

Introduce yourself. Tell what kind of animal you are—make up a good name for yourself. Tell what you look like, what parts and features of five different animals you have. Describe your unusual habits . . . things you do, what you eat, the noises you make, or whatever makes you *NEW TO THE ZOO!*

PICTURE THIS!

Draw a picture of the strange new animal you've described above. Be sure to put the name of the animal under the picture.

IMAGINE THAT . . .

. . . All of a sudden for some unknown reason you are highly allergic to other people!

THINK ABOUT/TALK ABOUT:

1. How might you have gotten such an unusual allergy?

2. What might your allergic reaction be—sneezing, hives, something weird or funny? Describe what happens whenever you're near other people now that you have this allergy.

3. What kind of problems would such an allergy cause?

4. Are there some people you wouldn't mind being allergic to? Why?

5. How could you solve the problem of having such an allergy and still be able to have contact with the people you like?

WRITE ABOUT . . .

ACHOO! I'M ALLERGIC TO YOU!

Tell what happened the day you came to school even though you were highly allergic to other people. Tell about the problems you faced and how you solved them. Tell how other people reacted to your allergy, how they tried to help you (or make you more miserable). Try to come up with a really original ending—a good way to either live with the problem or solve it, or a unique way to cure such a unique allergy.

PICTURE THIS!

Draw a picture of what happens to you while you have this allergy and how you get close to another person.

IMAGINE THAT...

... All the computers have united and have taken over the world!

THINK ABOUT/TALK ABOUT:

1. How would you, as a human, feel about computers taking over?

2. Would there be any advantages to having computers instead of people in control of the world?

3. What would be the disadvantages and problems of having computers in control?

4. What might have made the computers angry enough to take over?

5. What could you and the other humans do about the computer revolt?

WRITE ABOUT...

THE GREAT COMPUTER WAR!

You have been hired by the President to take charge of the war against the computers. It's up to you to come up with a plan to conquer the computers and put people back in control of the world. Describe your plan and tell if it does or doesn't work. Do you win the Great Computer War or do the computers keep control?

PICTURE THIS!

Suppose the computers stay in charge and they've just elected their first computer president of the country. Draw a picture of that first computer president. Give him/her a personality and a good computer president name.

IMAGE THAT . . .

. . . An evil witch has just put a spell on you!

THINK ABOUT/TALK ABOUT:

1. What might you have done to make the witch angry enough to put the spell on you in the first place?

2. What did she say and do in casting the spell?

3. What kind of spell was it? What did it do to you?

4. How do you feel about the spell? What kind of problems might it cause you?

5. How might you go about convincing the witch to remove the spell?

WRITE ABOUT . . .

MIS-SPELLED!

Tell the story of the day (or night) that a witch put a spell on you. Describe the witch and how you felt when you saw her. Tell why she put a spell on you. Tell what the spell did to you and what you did about it. Tell what happened while you were under the spell. And see if you can come up with a good way to undo the spell, either on your own or by getting the witch to undo it. Tell the story of the day an evil witch mis-spelled you!

PICTURE THIS!

Draw a picture of the witch who cast the spell OR of yourself while you were under her spell.

IMAGINE THAT . . .

. . . You are a piece of equipment used in your favorite sport!

THINK ABOUT/TALK ABOUT:

1. What is your favorite sport? Why? Do you like to play this sport, watch it, or both?

2. Which piece of equipment would you choose to be? Why?

3. How would you feel about the way you are used in the game? Proud? Afraid? Annoyed? etc.

4. How do you feel about the people who play your sport? What makes them special? Why?

5. What kind of personality would such a piece of equipment probably have? What would be a suitable name?

WRITE ABOUT . . .

THE . . . . .REVOLT!

(Fill in the blank with the kind of equipment you've chosen to be, for example, football's, tennis racket's, baseball bat's, hockey puck's, sneakers, etc. to complete the title.)

Imagine that you are a piece of sporting equipment used in your favorite sport. The only trouble is you're tired of the way you're used and treated. You think people who play your sport take you for granted, so you're going to teach them a lesson. You're just not going to cooperate today. You're going to do everything wrong, make everything turn out different than it should, really mix up the game. Tell what you do . . . and how the players react to the revolt.

PICTURE THIS!

Draw a picture of yourself as a piece of sporting equipment. Give yourself a personality and a name.

IMAGINE THAT . . .

. . . You are a star in a traveling circus!

THINK ABOUT/TALK ABOUT:

1. What kind of an act would you have? Would it be funny or thrilling?

2. What kind of costume would you wear?

3. How would you like traveling from town to town putting on the show? Would you like it or not? Why?

4. What would be the best things about being a circus star and living with the circus?

5. How would your family feel if you told them you wanted to join the circus?

WRITE ABOUT . . .

UNDER THE BIG TOP!

The big top circus tent is full. The ringmaster has just announced your name. The crowd claps and cheers. You are famous! They have been waiting to see your act. You step into the center ring, and . . .

Tell about your act in the circus. Tell what you do, how you feel about it, how the crowd reacts, how you feel about their applause (or boos!), if your act goes well or something unexpected happens, how your acts end, and what the crowd does as you leave the ring.

PICTURE THIS!

Draw a picture of yourself in your circus star costume.

IMAGE THAT . . .

. . . You are the mother or father of a dozen children!

THINK ABOUT/TALK ABOUT:

1. What would be the problems with having a dozen children?

2. What would be good about such a large family?

3. What kind of house would you need? What special features would it need to have?

4. How would you feel about taking care of so many children?

5. What do you think is the ideal number of children for a family to have? Why?

WRITE ABOUT . . .

KIDS BY THE DOZEN!

Describe a typical morning at your house with you and your dozen kids . . . everybody getting up and washed and dressed, fixing breakfasts, getting off to work and school on time. How do the children help out? How do they get along? How do you figure out who does what, who gets the bathroom first, etc? Describe your typical morning!

PICTURE THIS!

Draw a family portrait of your dozen children. Make them as different as you can with distinct features, sizes and ages. Give each child a name.

IMAGINE THAT . . .

. . . A magician has given you the opportunity to change your age to any age that you choose!

THINK ABOUT/TALK ABOUT:

1. What are the advantages and disadvantages of your present age?

2. What would be the advantages and disadvantages of being younger?

3. What would be the advantages and disadvantages of being older?

4. What do you think would be the perfect age? Why?

5. What would you do after the magician changed your age?

WRITE ABOUT . . .

ABRACADABRA! ALACAZAM! WHAT AGE DO YOU THINK I AM?

Think of the age you would ask the magician to make you. Now list at least five things under each heading below. Then, without telling anyone what age you've chosen, show your list to several of your classmates. See if anybody can guess the age YOU think is perfect. See if you can guess what age they would want to be.

1. Things I can can do at this age that I can't do now.
2. Things I'd be too old to do.
3. Things I'd be too young to do.
4. Things I wouldn't have to do anymore if I were this new age.
5. Best things about being the age I've chosen.
6. Worst things about being the age I've chosen.

What age do you think I am?

PICTURE THIS!

Draw something you could do at your new age that you can't do now.

IMAGE THAT . . .

. . . You are the world's only talking sneaker!

THINK ABOUT/TALK ABOUT:

1. What would you think of having to run around on someone's foot all day?

2. How would you feel about the person who wore you?

3. What would be the worst part of a sneaker's life?

4. What might your owner do with you that would make you angry?

5. What would be the perfect name for a talking sneaker?

WRITE ABOUT . . .

THE SNEAKER SPEAKER

The speaker at today's assembly program is a little unusual—the world's only talking sneaker! Suppose *you* are that sneaker speaker. Write the speech you would give to the students in your class. What would you tell them about being a sneaker? How would you tell them a sneaker should be treated? What complaints would you make—what advice would you give? This is your chance to speak up for all the sneakers of the world!

PICTURE THIS!

Draw *your version* of the world's only talking sneaker!